£1. B.

- Visitors with disabilities: this is a large open-air museum with many period buildings and some steep slopes. Visitors in wheelchairs are advised to be accompanied. A free leaflet to assist visitors with disabilities is available at Admissions in the Entrance Building.

- First Aid: if you need assistance, please speak to any member of staff.

- Dogs should be kept on leads and must be accompanied at all times. They are not allowed into any building (with the exception of guide dogs).

- Smoking is not permitted in any of the buildings or refreshment areas, or on any vehicles.

- Please do not take food or drink into any period building.

- There are public telephones in the tearooms and entrance building.

- Photography: visitors are welcome to make videos and take photographs for their personal use only. Written permission is required for photography for any other use.

A winter visit is centred on the Town and Tramway only. Other areas of the museum are closed in winter and, consequently, admission charges are reduced.

All period exhibits close fifteen minutes before the advertised closing time of the museum. The last tram leaves the Town and Pockerley Manor fifteen minutes before the advertised closing time of the museum. The last guided tour of the Drift Mine is half an hour before the advertised closing time of the museum.

Contents

D0260108

Introduction

Beamish is a treasure house of the North East. Our internationally renowned collections are wide, varied and extensive. Our aim is to portray something of the life and work of northern people, at two key points in the region's history, the 1820s and 1913. You won't see objects in isolation, you'll see them in their everyday setting and what's more, you'll see someone using them. Someone who'll be happy to tell you, where, when, why and how!

The Museum is constantly changing. We continually strive to collect, research and rebuild so that we can preserve more of the region's past way of life, before it disappears for ever. Many of our visitors return again and again, and each time absorb just a little more of the spirit of Beamish.

Beamish is a tribute to the people of the North East, and owes its existence to them and their continued support. So much is special at this great Museum – the vast collections on which it is based, the knowledge and research which has painstakingly recreated and furnished each building and setting, the valley in which it is set and, most of all, the people who bring it to life. Each one has a skill to share and a tale to tell.

I hope that you'll enjoy Beamish and take away a deeper understanding of the North East, its people and its fascinating past, along with many happy memories of your visit.

Miriam Harte
Director

History

The beginnings of Beamish go back to 1970, when Frank Atkinson, first Director and founder, and his small band of colleagues first came to Beamish. The idea, however, to establish an 'open air museum' of the Scandinavian type goes back to 1958, when Frank had just been

appointed Director of the Bowes Museum at Barnard Castle, a museum largely concerned with continental, fine and applied art. Frank's interests were much wider than this. He realised that the North East region was changing dramatically, the old industries of coal-mining, shipbuilding and iron and steel manufacture were disappearing along with the communities that served them. "It is essential" he said, "that collecting be carried out quickly and on as big a scale as possible. It is now almost too late."

Top: Brancepeth camp – store for collections
Above left: Collecting exhibits
Above right: Beamish No 2 winding engine on original site
Above: Gateshead No 10 tram in town street
Below: Frank Atkinson with sign post collection

He was most concerned that the region was losing its identity, "customs, traditions and ways of speech" were dying out. Frank proposed that the new museum would "illustrate vividly the way of life … of the ordinary people", and would "attempt to make the history of the region live".

Urgency was the watchword. Frank adopted a policy of "unselective collecting … you offer it to us and we will collect it". The imagination of the people of the region was captured and they donated objects of all sizes, from steam engines to shops and sewing machines. A whole army camp of 22 huts and hangars at Brancepeth was rapidly filled, creating a bond between museum and community, which has never been lost.

A group of Friends actively collected for and supported the idea of the museum and eventually, after much discussion and argument, the politicians of the region representing eight local authorities within the North East, agreed to a joint financial and management arrangement. The search was then on for a suitable site. A basin-shaped valley of about 300 acres, with steep slopes, a river, woodland areas, some level ground and a south-facing aspect, was thought to be ideal. Beamish, one of many sites considered and once the home of the Shafto and Eden families, was available and was ideal for the purpose, having buildings of some antiquity already in situ. The land was acquired and the rest is history.

1968
Friends of Beamish formed

1970
Museum established

1971
First Exhibition – Museum in the Making

1973
Home Farm acquired

1976
Rowley Station officially opened by Poet Laureate Sir John Betjeman – first building moved to Beamish

1985
Town Street officially opened by HRH Duke of Gloucester

1987
Museum voted Museum of Europe

1995
Pockerley Manor opens – the 1820s area is established

1997
Museum's collections designated as being of outstanding importance

1999
Pockerley Waggonway opens

2001
Regional Resource Centre opens

2002
Regional Museums Store completed
Launch of the *Steam Elephant*

2003
Launch of Sunderland Tram 16

2006
Launch of Puffing Billy
Opening of Masonic Hall

The early 19th century was a period of great potential, though also of social turmoil. After the French Revolution, Britain had been at war with France; Nelson was dead, having won his famous battle at Trafalgar, and Napoleon had been defeated at the Battle of Waterloo in 1815. At home the nation which George IV ruled was a restless one with plots and rebellions throughout the realm.

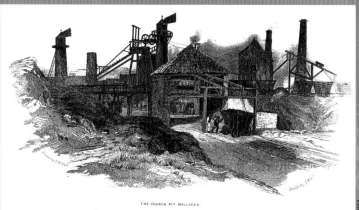

THE CHURCH PIT WALLSEND.

Britain, however, led the world in the production of coal, lead, iron, chemicals, glass, pottery and textiles. Shipbuilding was also coming into its own, though real growth in the region was not seen until the 1850s.

Top: Making oatcakes.
Walker's Costumes
of Yorkshire 1813
Middle: Jubilee Pit,
Coxlodge,
Thomas Hair 1839
Above: Church Pit,
Wallsend,
Thomas Hair 1839
Above left:
Tees-water old breed,
Thomas Bewick
Left: From "The
Collier's Wedding"
by Edward Chicken

The North East pioneered in agricultural developments, particularly in livestock breeding. The Culley brothers and Colling brothers introduced new ideas of stock breeding and by the 1820s Northumberland, especially, and Durham were being held up, by the Improvers as examples of the 'new farming'. Shorthorn cattle that were bred in the region were exported all over the country.

In the North East, coal production in the 18th century had been concentrated along the banks of the Rivers Tyne and Wear, where the pits were relatively shallow and transport via river to sea was easy. As these seams were

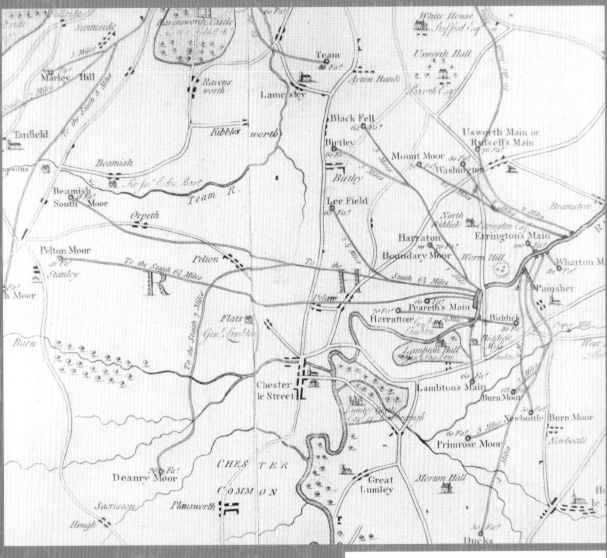

exhausted or flooded, improved pumping methods and the development of the safety lamp allowed for a rapid increase in the number of pits being sunk to a great depth and also further inland.

The increased demand for coal led to the development of waggonways and pit communities, which sprang up seemingly overnight throughout the North East. It was these early waggonways or 'coal roads' that the Stockton and Darlington Railway was built to replace. Opened in 1825, it was the world's first public steam-hauled passenger railway, its success leading to the rapid adoption of railways through the country and the world.

Above: Early map
Right: Coal Certificate
Below: Waggonway from John Gibson's Plan of the Collieries 1788

1801
Middlesbrough has population of 25 people

1803
Cornishman Richard Trevithick tests the first railway locomotive

1805
First railway locomotive in the North East

1810
George III declared insane

1811
George, Prince of Wales, becomes Prince Regent

1813
Puffing Billy and *Wylam Dilly* locomotives built by William Hedley

1815
Steam Elephant built
Miner's safety lamp invented by Humphry Davy and George Stephenson

1820
Prince Regent becomes George IV

1822
World's first pedigree herdbook published recording the Durham Shorthorn

1825
Opening of the Stockton and Darlington Railway

1827
Newcastle to London by stagecoach non stop in 36 hours

1830
George IV dies and William IV succeeds

1837
William IV dies and Queen Victoria succeeds

Pockerley Manor

1825

APG

**Above: Pockerley
Manor House
Left: 68th Regiment
of Foot**

The Beamish valley has a long and fascinating history. 'Boldon Buke', the great rental carried out by Bishop Hugh Pudsey of Durham in 1183, makes reference to Pockerley and there are signs of an ancient defensive site – evidence of a far from peaceful past. The Reivers, both Scots and English, once ravaged this countryside from where the word 'blackmail' originated.

Here a medieval strong house was built with vaulted undercroft, still retaining its original roof timbers of the 1440s.

94128

The newer manor house, with its Georgian windows and red pantiled roof dates back to about 1720. The house, gardens and farm buildings are of a kind that typically would be owned by a yeoman farmer and landowner.

The south-facing terraces contain a formal parterre garden, a cultivated vegetable garden and orchards. The plants, shrubs and tree species here were listed in the catalogues published by William Falla, whose nurseries in Gateshead in the 1820s covered 600 acres and were the largest in the kingdom. They have proved invaluable for our research on which all interpretation has been based.

83380

Top : Early 1800s engraving of coach and four
Above: Sampler by Jane Bradley 1814

Pockerley Manor

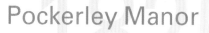

65017

The manor house is shown as it would have been in the 1820s, when a yeoman landowner, along with his family, servants and labourers, ran the surrounding farm estate. The **back kitchen** has a peat fire. Note the slab of Frosterley marble and large stone sink where the clothes were washed, dishes cleaned and food prepared. A plunger churn was used for butter making, whilst other tools were used for peat-cutting, pig killing, sheep clipping and net repairs.

The **pantry** on the north side of the house is well ventilated and painted with limewash to discourage flies and bugs. Salt fish, pheasants, rabbits and a turkey hang from the hooks. Here also are stored soap, candles, pickles, preserves and fresh herbs and vegetables.

The **large kitchen** is the most important room in the house. In the 1820s cooking ranges were only just being introduced, although the well established beehive bread-oven would be in daily use.

A large pine table with sycamore top was used by the extended family and servants for main meals. The kitchen furniture is mostly of oak, the dresser displaying pewter plates and Spode blue-and-white pottery. An unusual long case clock has a face painted by Beilby and Hawthorn, with a colliery scene typical of the period.

The **parlour** has elegant painted pine panelling and provincial

59197

**Top left: The Pantry
Left: Silhouette of
S. Hodges 1826
Below: Purse frame
c 1480 – 1520, found
during excavations
at Pockerley
Above: Main kitchen
Right: Master bedroom**

101921

80440

65047

country-style furniture, whilst the family's interests in stock-breeding can be seen in the fine portraits of Durham Shorthorns, the Northumberland Ox and a Chestnut Arabian stallion.

A **master bedroom** has a four-poster Georgian bedstead with chintz hangings and real linen bedclothes. Most of the prints and pictures in the room relate to rural life but also include portraits of 'Capability' Brown and Master Lambton – the Red Boy.

The smaller bedroom next door, with its arsenic green wallpaper could well have been used for a child.

1825

The servants and farm labourers slept in smaller, darker, north-facing rooms at the back of the house, whilst the family occupied sunnier rooms at the front. Single servants would 'live in', though males and females were strictly segregated. Note the scant furnishings, lack of fires and absence of privacy. Married servants always 'lived out'. The stronghouse could well have been occupied by a married hind or farm labourer.

One main living room accommodated the fine oak box bed, dating back to 1712, though still very typical of the period. A superb wrought iron chimney crane hangs over the fire. From time to time there are demonstrations of tallow candle making and spinning.

Horses provided the main means of transport in the early 1800s. The Georgian stables nearby are home to the estate's Clydesdales, Cleveland Bays and Dales ponies. A Dales pony regularly travels the pack-horse route which passes through the farmyard and around the valley.

Far left: Watercolour of Chestnut Arabian horse, c 1803
Above: Chimney crane and hearth in the old house
Below left: Gardens at Pockerley
Right: Pack horse and driver

The Georgian Landscape

The museum is recreating, around Pockerley, a landscape typical of the 1820s period, when enclosures, collieries and early railways and waggonways were changing the face of the North East. Fields were laid out in a series of ridges and furrows, prior to the invention of tile drains and mechanised farm machinery.

Ridge and furrow is of particular interest in emphasising the different conditions between the ridges (dry) and furrows (wet), which once established a much greater grass and plant variation.

Lost fence lines are being replaced with riven oak fences to allow the land to be grazed in more traditional fields. The museum will also recreate early industrial and rural communities including a village with watermill and water powered forge. The millponds and millraces which once existed around the Beamish valley in the early 1800s will be restored.

A horse waggonway has been constructed following the contours across the fields below Pockerley. The waggon-way leads towards a small early colliery

Left: *Steam Elephant* loco and railway cutting through the Georgian landscape
Top: "A coal waggon" watercolour sketch by John Dixon 1783
Above: Pockerley Manor and landscape
Right: "Representation of a horse gin" from John Holland's *Fossil Fuel* 1835
Below right: "A Newcastle Coal Pit" from Matthias Dunn's *Winning & Working of Collieries* 1848

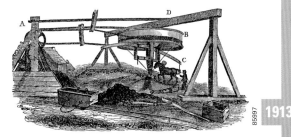

with its waste heap and horse gin for winding coal, once a common feature of northern landscapes of the period. This area illustrates the story of the emergence of a large scale mining industry.

Pockerley Waggonway

In the valley below Pockerley Manor runs the Pockerley Waggonway. Horse waggonways had existed in the North East since the 17th century. The rails were normally made of wood, though after 1800 their character started to change when iron rails became increasingly popular. Locomotives were tried and stationary steam engines were used to haul waggons with cables.

Top: Bothy for engine drivers and waggonway men
Right: Old egg ended boiler used as a platform shelter
Below right: Engine shed with Locomotion and waggons

All the waggonways in the region were built to move coal from pit to riverside. By 1815 over 2½ million tons of coal were being transported to the Tyne or the Wear.

It was in the North East that nearly all the early experiments with locomotives were tried out between 1812 and 1825, culminating in the building of George Stephenson's *Locomotion No 1* for the Stockton and Darlington Railway. It was George Stephenson (1781–1848) who took the credit for much of this work, however, other engineers played an equally important part in this early experimentation. It is certainly not true that George Stephenson 'invented' the locomotive.

REA162

The Great Shed at the Waggonway is based upon the lost buildings of Timothy Hackworth's works at Shildon, County Durham. Incorporated in the structure is original iron work from George Stephenson's Forth Bank works in Newcastle upon Tyne. Here can be

seen information on other engineers working at the period. A bothy, or workmen's rest room, encourages visitors to sit by the fire. Visitors may also have the opportunity to experience steam-hauled travel in unsprung recreated carriages, the enclosed one similar to that first used on the opening day of the S & D Railway.

Above: Locomotion taking on water at the Stanhope & Tyne watercrane
Left: Watercolour of a Blenkinsop locomotive c 1813
Below left: 68th Regiment of Foot re-enactment

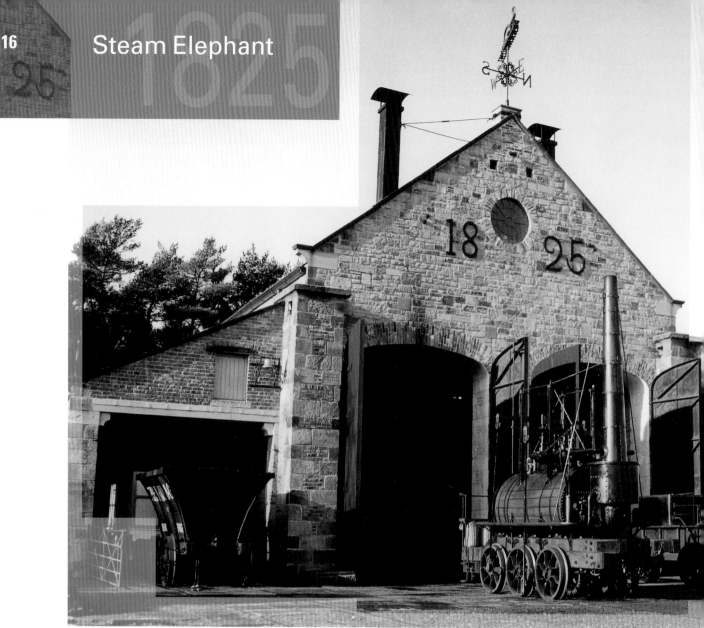

One of the museum's most exciting recent discoveries was an unknown oil painting of a very early locomotive of 1815, called the *Steam Elephant*. It was designed by locomotive pioneer William Chapman for John Buddle, the most famous viewer and mining engineer of his day, known as the 'King of Coal Trade'. Built for Wallsend Colliery, parts of the engine were machined by Hawks foundry of Gateshead.

No original design drawings for the *Steam Elephant* have survived, though there exists a remarkable series of sketches of it. Exhaustive researches by the museum's staff have rewritten the history of early railways and have made it possible to produce a detailed design for the engine with some 200 blueprints and specifications, from which the replica has

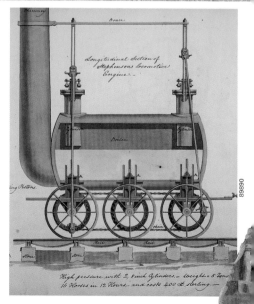

Left, above and top right: Details, including Stephenson's patent locomotive of 1825, from a document of that date, by William Strickland, an American spy sent to report back on transport and industrial development

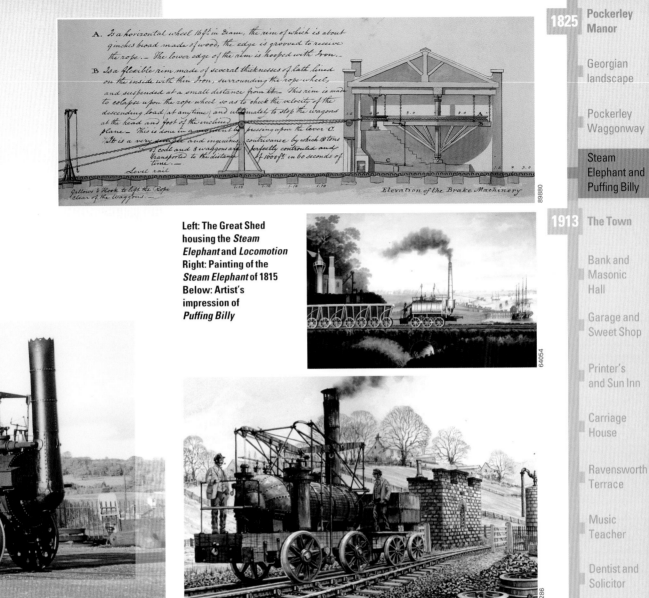

A. Is a horizontal wheel 16 ft in diam, the rim of which is about 9 inches broad made of wood, the edge is grooved to receive the rope. — The lower edge of the rim is hooped with Iron. —

B. Is a flexible rim made of several thicknesses of lath lined on the inside with their Iron, surrounding the rope wheel, and suspended at a small distance from the — This rim is made to collapse upon the rope-wheel so as to check the velocity of the descending load (at anytime) and ultimately to stop the waggons at the head and foot of the inclined plane. — This is done in a moment by pressing upon the lever C. It is a very simple and ingenious contrivance by which 18 tons of coal and 8 waggons are perfectly controuled and transported to the distance of 1000 ft in 60 seconds of time. — Level rail

Gallows & Hook to lift the Rope clear of the Waggons.

Elevation of the Brake Machinery.

89880

Left: The Great Shed housing the *Steam Elephant* and *Locomotion*
Right: Painting of the *Steam Elephant* of 1815
Below: Artist's impression of *Puffing Billy*

64054

91286

Below: Typical early 1800s colliery scene with horse gin, along the river Tyne. Painted by Beilby and Hawthorn on the lunette of a long case clock by Weston of Wolsingham *c* 1814, in Pockerley Manor

been built. Modern safety brakes have been added to ensure it can be operated to carry passengers safely – an amazing project successfully accomplished.

The museum's next challenge was to design and build a working replica of *Puffing Billy*, one of the world's oldest surviving locomotives, built in 1813 by William Hedley and now in the Science Museum in London. The replica can now be seen at Beamish, in steam from time to time.

1913

Mineral wealth was the source of the region's economic growth.

By 1896 Teesside was producing almost a third of the nation's iron output. Essential ingredients for Victorian industrial growth were iron and steel for rail track, for locomotives, for steam engines and for bridges and ships. The shipyards on the Tyne and Wear were producing two-thirds of the national tonnage.

The 19th century saw a large influx of labour into the region, to work in the mines and to operate furnaces and

factory machinery. Coal was used to fire the furnaces, the furnaces made the iron, the iron built the ships and the ships transported the coal. People came, not only from the Northumbrian countryside, but also from Cumberland,

Top: River Wear at Sunderland with coal drops in the foreground
Above left: Postcard from W Stanley Disaster 1909
Above right: King Street, South Shields 1890 with horse tram
Right: Quarries at Springwell, Gateshead
Below: Blue Bell Pit, Backworth

Scotland, Ireland, Yorkshire and Cornwall. They brought with them their own dialects, habits and customs and were integrated into the local communities. They have left their mark on the North East in culture and tradition and in producing that identifiable character which is uniquely North Eastern.

Rapid economic development brought not only wealth, but also social problems. The expansion of industry created problems of poor housing, public health and working conditions, both in urban and rural areas. Depopulation of the countryside caused abandonment of some isolated farms, and a downward creep of the moorland boundaries.

The period between 1900 and 1913 was of particular importance in the history of the North East, which played a vital part in the national economy on several fronts. In 1913 production was at its peak in the Great Northern Coalfield, and by 1914 a substantial proportion of British and World trade was taken by the North East.

Top: The Alnwick & Berwick Garage, Berwick on Tweed
Above: Stephenson's Manufactory in Newcastle upon Tyne
Left: Launch of SS Grantala, 1903 built by W G Armstrong Whitworth
Left middle: Boats in Cullercoats bay
Below: Bill Hall ploughing at Whitehall Farm near Rowley

1901
Queen Victoria dies and Edward VII succeeds

Middlesbrough has population of 91,302 people

1902
Boer War ends

1903
Smallpox epidemic hits Newcastle

1906
Doxford ship builders produce one ship every two weeks

1908
First Model T Ford car produced in Detroit

Old Age Pension introduced

1909
168 men and boys killed in West Stanley pit disaster

1910
George V ascends to throne

1913
Suffragette Emily Davison, killed by throwing herself in front of the King's Horse at the Derby

1913
Peak year of coal production in the Great Northern coalfield

1914
Britain declares war on Germany – beginning of First World War

The Town represents a typical north-eastern market town of the years leading up to the First World War. The region's towns grew rapidly from the 1870s onwards, with some seeing considerable improvements in sanitation, water supply, street lighting and other amenities. The results of many of these changes can be seen here.

At the west end of the Town is a Victorian park with ornamental flower beds and a bandstand, by Walter MacFarlane & Co. of Glasgow, originally from Saltwell Park in Gateshead. Brass band concerts are held here on some Sundays during the summer season. Municipal parks were a typical feature of

Above: The 1913 Town street
Left: Groom and carriage horse

1	Masonic Hall and Bank	6	Carriage house
2	Sweet Shop	7	Ravensworth Terrace
3	The Garage	8	The Solicitor
4	Printer's	9	The Dentist
5	The Sun Inn	10	The Co-op

32938

80463

1825 **Pockerley Manor**

Georgian landscape

Pockerley Waggonway

Steam Elephant and Puffing Billy

1913 **The Town**

Bank and Masonic Hall

Garage and Sweet Shop

Printer's and Sun Inn

Carriage House

Ravensworth Terrace

Music Teacher

...st and ...itor

...Co-op ...Dainty ...h

...Station ...RMS

...ms and ...nsport

...3 Home Farm

1913 **Colliery Village**

Pit Cottages

School and Chapel

The Colliery

turning electric motors, operating tram cars and heating ovens and radiators.

One of the most remarkable features of the period was the rapid expansion of tramway systems, which provided cheap transport for working people. By 1913 motor cars were also gaining a reputation for sound construction and reliability and production line cars were being manufactured in this country for the first time.

Top: Detail from Park bandstand
Above: Bandstand originally from Saltwell Park in Gateshead

96339

Victorian towns. Where housing conditions were often insanitary and overcrowded, the park provided an opportunity for exercise, fresh air and entertainment.

In the early years of the 19th century, many towns were beginning to have their own supplies of gas and it was especially for public street lighting that gas was first produced. The North East led the way in the introduction of electric power for lighting and it was not long before it was being used for

Left: From the catalogue of Walter MacFarlane

29552

Above: Main banking hall in Barclay & Co bank
Right: In the bank manager's office
Below: Exterior of Town bank

96565

96566

The Bank Barclay & Company was formed in 1896 by the amalgamation of some 20 private banks. The large north-eastern banks, Backhouse and Company, Woods and Company and J W Pease and Company, were part of the new grouping. The new bank had strong links with Quaker business and finance dynasties.

The local Head Office was in Darlington and most of the Directors had been partners in Backhouses. Most major banking decisions were still taken in the region rather than in London. Personal accounts were only a small part of the Bank's business compared to today.

The Bank is a fine four-storey building designed to give its customers a feeling of financial stability and security.

The 'Swedish Imperial Red' granite frontage is typical of banks of the period. The upper storeys have been assembled from bricks and quoins saved from Park House, Gateshead.

The banking hall is the best surviving example of the period. Downstairs visitors can take a peep into the vaults.

15566

Above: Interior of Park Terrace, Masonic Hall c 1889
Right: Procession of Freemasons 1st July 2000
Far right top: Early watercolour of Freemason, South Shields 1821
Far middle: Sunderland ware jug with Masonic symbols
Far middle: Masonic jewels from a trade catalogue
Far bottom: Artist's impression of Bank and Masonic Hall

The Masonic Hall In 1913, Freemasonry formed an integral part of society, taking part in Masonic processions was one of the many aspects of community life. Now a Masonic Hall will take its place next to the Bank enabling all our visitors to see inside a typical meeting place and to find out more about Freemasonry.

With the assistance of the Provincial Grand Lodge of Durham, the museum has saved the frontage of the former Park Terrace Masonic Hall at Sunderland, originally built in 1869.

The Hall had been in use until 1932 when it was replaced by the new Wearside Masonic Hall.

The foundation stone was laid on 1st July 2000, and on 19th April 2006, some 2000 freemasons in full regalia processed along the Town street to witness the official opening of the Hall by HRH The Duke of Kent.

GEORGE KENNING, LONDON, LIVERPOOL, MANCHESTER, & GLASGOW.
28

Garage and Sweet Shop

96567

Top: Garage showroom with Renault car
Above: Calendar print – "We shall be wanted yet"
Below: Armstrong Whitworth car of 1907

80452

The Garage The Beamish Motor and Cycle Works is a typical town garage of the pre-First World War period. This Edwardian building fits the early requirements of *The Cycle and Motor Trade Review*, which praised a garage as "a shop for the supply of the motorist's numerous accessories … an engineering works … and care and shelter for the complete car". Early garages combined the skills of the blacksmith, wheelwright and coachbuilder. Petrol was supplied not from pumps, but in two-gallon cans.

The showroom displays new and second-hand cars, motorcycles and bicycles. Headlamps and horns were supplied as extras. A variety of vehicles is shown, notably the expensive and rare Armstrong Whitworth car of 1907, made in Newcastle upon Tyne, a pre-war Renault and a Model T Ford nicknamed the 'Tin Lizzy'. A Dene motorcycle of 1912 is a rare survivor from the works in Newcastle.

In 1913 there was little standardisation of spare parts. Most were made or remade in the workshop. Lighting sets, gas, electric or acetylene were supplied separately. Over the pit under repair, can be seen a unique survivor from the Seaham Harbour Engine Works. The SHEW was originally built in 1906 as an articulated car – a one off for the company.

Garages of this size hired out charabancs and were often haulage contractors. To the rear of the Garage is a Daimler wagon being used for a house removal.

Rowntree's Assorted Chocolates

45163

FRY'S MILK CHOCOLATE
MAKERS TO H M THE KING • 300 GOLD MEDALS &c
2 FOR 2½d

46118

The Sweet Shop

The tremendous variety of sweets on offer today has only become available during the last hundred years.

Once chocolate was drunk by the privileged few. In the 19th century the combination of sugar and cocoa revolutionised the confectionery trade and led to chocolate being made specifically for eating. Improvements in mechanisation and distribution created a growing market. The firms of Fry's, Terry's, Cadbury's and Rowntree's were pioneers in this expansion.

Inside, the Jubilee Confectioner's has fine mahogany fittings, mirrors and shelves packed with traditional glass jars full of sugared almonds, black bullets and sour plums.

In the factory behind the shop,

62830a

Top left and right: Sweet wrappers from Rowntree's and Fry's, two of the main chocolate firms
Above: The sweetshop selling hardboiled sweets

ROWNTREE'S IMPERIAL CHOCOLATES.
46118

visitors can experience the whole process of traditional sweet making, see the sugar being boiled in huge copper boiling pans, and watch the sugar rollers cutting the sweets into different shapes of bullets, stars and fishes. They can then be bought in the shop.

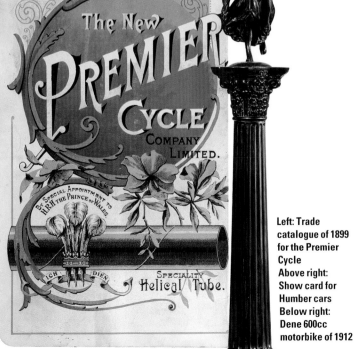

1899
The New PREMIER CYCLE COMPANY LIMITED.
BY SPECIAL APPOINTMENT TO H.R.H THE PRINCE OF WALES
ICH DIEN
SPECIALITY Helical Tube.

HUMBER CARS

SV 7712

Left: Trade catalogue of 1899 for the Premier Cycle
Above right: Show card for Humber cars
Below right: Dene 600cc motorbike of 1912

The Printer's Across the street from the Co-op Store, the news headlines for 1913 are prominently displayed outside the branch office of a local newspaper. The office was a distribution point: newspapers printed at Head Office on high-speed presses were distributed to branch offices to be sold over the counter in newsagents and by street-sellers. It also acted as a base for a local reporter to report the latest stories by telephone, the new technology in 1913.

Top: Stationer's shop and newspaper branch office
Left: Columbian Press No 766 of 1837

Advertising copy could also be left at the downstairs counter.

Upstairs a jobbing printer produced posters, business cards, advertising material and private and commercial stationery for local customers. For short runs the Arab Platen Press was used. For more extensive orders and posters the fast semi-automatic Wharfedale Press was employed. At the rear of the print shop stands the magnificently ornamented early Victorian Columbian Press, easily identifiable by its gilt eagle.

Downstairs the shop stocks a range of specially selected cards, prints and copies of Edwardian stationery. Look out for the writing materials bearing familiar household names of Reeves, Rowney, Waterman's and Conway-Stewart.

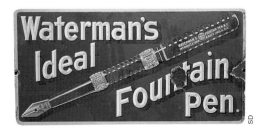

WILLSHER'S
BLACK BULL
SPECIAL SCOTCH WHISKY
DUNDEE

"King George IV"
Whisky
Distillers Company Ltd.
Edinburgh.

PUCK ✦ CAPTAIN WEBB ✦ MATCHES

ALFRED BIRD'S GINGER BEER POWDER

The Sun Inn, originally from High Bondgate in Bishop Auckland, dates back to the 1860s, although there had been an earlier pub named the Tiger on this site. The interior has been altered many times, but at Beamish, it has been rebuilt much as it was originally with the 'Bar' and 'Select'. The magnificent glass mirrors, a feature of the pub, have been

Left: Match holder and striker
Below: The bar in the Sun Inn

collected over the years along with other typical furnishings. Draught beers and lager, very much the new drink in 1913, are sold.

J.A. ANDERSON
2/6
FINE OLD GIN
WHOLESALE SPIRIT MERCHANT
MORPETH

BASS & Cᵒˢ
GREEN SEAL
Per 3/- Doz
LARGE BOTTLES
BRILLIANT ALE

ROBERTSON SANDERSONS
MOUNTAIN DEW
GIN

JOHN WALKER & SONS
KILMARNOCK WHISKY

80458

Carriage House and Horses

Through the archway adjoining the Sun Inn are the **Town Stables** and **Carriage House**. In 1913 the main form of transport was still the horse, and most inns and pubs had stables associated with them. Some were small catering for a couple of travellers' horses, while other yards developed into major enterprises with stables, vehicles for hire, general livestock feed suppliers and what we would now call transport contractors.

Before the coming of the railways, posting or coaching establishments were essential. A coach would exchange horses every 12–14 miles. By 1913 trains, buses and cars were competing with horses but

Top left: Carriage house
Above: Rington's Tea van of *c* 1907
Left: Carriage horses

most local transport and deliveries were achieved with horse drawn vehicles.

The stables are quite large, accommodating the museum's coach horses. The harness room, with fittings from Callaly Castle in Northumberland, displays both working and exhibition

Above and left: Carriage house with variety of horse drawn vehicles, shoeing forge and foreman's office
Below left: Old photo of McIntyres's carriage works at Durham

harness – the wonderful crested driving harness was used in 1897 at Queen Victoria's Diamond Jubilee celebrations. Period adverts, post horns, riding boots, early prints and prizes give a flavour of the period.

Next to the Stables, is the Carriage House with its unusual cast-iron roof trusses of the 1840s. A foreman's office and 'shoeing forge' can be seen. Vehicle repairs and horse shoeing would be undertaken here. A splendid array of horse drawn vehicles can be seen including a North Eastern Railway rolley, Hoult's furniture removal van, Station omnibus, Park drag, Shand Mason steam fire engine, Hearse by Archibalds of Alnwick, and Ringtons Tea van, to mention only a few.

Ravensworth Terrace

80472

REA

96350

The fine row of Georgian style houses, **Ravensworth Terrace**, originally from Bensham in Gateshead, was built between 1830 and 1845. These were fashionable houses built for professional people and tradesmen. Once, they were occupied by such people as John Wilson Carmichael, the landscape and marine painter, William Collard, the engraver in the early 1830s, and later on by Alexander Gillies, Mayor of Gateshead. Here they illustrate the houses of a music teacher, dentist and solicitor.

No 2 Ravensworth Terrace represents the home of Miss Florence Smith, a teacher of singing, piano and elocution, who has inherited this house and its contents from her parents. She has made few changes and the house still has an old-fashioned feel, with furniture and furnishings from the earlier mid-Victorian period. Her home is lit by oil lamps.

The cluttered parlour with its drapes and heavy curtains, is where Miss Smith teaches her

Left: Kitchen of No 2
Right: Front room of No 2
Below right: Maid of all work
Below left: Staffordshire flatback ornament

33328

80475

pupils, charging sixpence for a lesson. The furniture is of good quality walnut and the fine balloon back chairs are by Sopwith, the renowned cabinet makers of Newcastle upon Tyne.

The kitchen floor is laid with stone flags and cooking is done on the early cast-iron range. The main bedrooms are full of heavy mahogany furniture. Note the large four-poster bed. There is no bathroom or water closet. Each bedroom would have its own washstand, the maid of all work carrying coals and water to each room.

80422

3950

The Dentist's

In 1913 Dentistry was a relatively new profession and was often practised from the dentist's own home. Tooth pullers still operated from local street markets. Most people only visited the dentist in cases of extreme necessity. At No 3 Ravensworth, the downstairs parlour is used as a waiting room and upstairs are the surgery, recovery room and technician's workshop. Anaesthetics tended to be unreliable, though nitrous oxide or laughing gas was used. The cost of an extraction was quite a deterrent and often only oil of cloves was used to dull the pain! The surgery is dominated by the cast-iron dental chair with dental drill which inevitably required precise drilling and footwork.

The technician's room was used for the preparation of dentures. Wax impressions were taken and plaster of Paris used to prepare models of teeth. It is noteworthy that, until 1921, any person however ignorant, could inform the public that they practised dentistry provided that the title 'dentist' was not used.

The upstairs corridor leads from the surgery to the dentist's own home, which

26227

Top right: "Tugging at an eye tooth" by George Cruikshank 1821
Left: Early 1900s tin toy car
Right: Nursery in No 4
Far right: Technician's workshop

80413

80420

Along the terrace is the **Solicitor's Office**, a tribute and memorial to Robert Spence Watson, a Quaker and solicitor by profession in Newcastle. One of the great men that hailed from Tyneside, he became a national figure in politics, education and the art of industrial negotiation. The office of J & R S Watson is typical of many legal practices of the early 1900s and is very old fashioned.

The partner's or principal's office is at the front of the house. On the partner's desk are documents tied up with pink ribbon. The solicitor acted as Registrar of Births, Marriages and Deaths.

Around the walls are deed boxes from prominent local families. The office is old fashioned even for 1913. Both offices have a distinctly Dickensian feel. There are no typewriters, telephones or duplicators, and even the clock has stopped.

was tastefully and elegantly furnished. A nursery at the front of the house is cheerfully furnished with toys of the period. The master bedroom is dominated by an Italian brass bedstead. A bathroom has been recently installed – a great improvement on earlier facilities.

Top: Principal's office in the Solicitor's
Above: Bedroom – No 4

The Co-op and Dainty Dinah

Above: Placing an order in the grocery dept
Right: Collar check cloth was used to make pitmen's waistcoats

The Co-operative movement revolutionised the lives of working class people. It gave them more control over the way they shopped for basic goods, ensuring always correct weights and measures, the purity of goods and, of course, it provided a dividend to members. The Co-op movement had its own factories, which produced everything from shirts to soap to furniture, in good working conditions – no more than an eight-hour working day.

The Co-op also had its own bank, its own insurance and building societies; it sent its own MPs to Westminster, provided reading rooms as well as venues for meetings and social functions. It also encouraged women's suffrage.

The **Co-operative Store** here came originally from nearby Annfield Plain and dates back in part to 1870. Now housing grocery, drapery and hardware departments, it represents a typical store of the period. The overhead Lamson-Paragon Cash system operates a series of hollow balls, which carry money via overhead rails to a central cash office where the cashier recorded all transactions for the Dividend.

80456

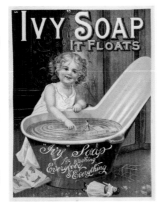

In the grocery department, most foods were weighed and packed by hand for each customer. Note the lentils, split peas and sugar, all in colour-coded paper bags. Butter was cut and patted into shape from large casks. Biscuits were sold loose. Branded pre-packed goods, were starting to appear. In relation to wages, food was more expensive for the average family in 1913 than it is today.

The drapery department stocked clothing and furnishing fabrics, haberdashery, a range of buttons, hooks, feathers, as well as collars, hats, shoes, gloves and other accessories. They also provided materials from which to make workmen's clothing such as pit hoggers.

The hardware department sold mangles, Pelaw Polish, paints, pots and pans, miners' lamps, picks, shovels and candles. The pitmen had to provide all their own gear.

Co-op prices were rarely the cheapest but the goods were reliable and the dividend was very welcome. The Co-op was renowned for providing 'Everything from the cradle to the grave'.

Above right: Hardware dept
Below: A typical Co-operative store

80457

TEA ROOMS ☞

Dainty Dinah
Whilst visiting the Town, don't forget to call in to the Dainty Dinah Tearooms, situated above the Co-operative Store on the Town Street. Taking its name from the famous Dainty Dinah toffee manufactured by Horner's of Chester-le-Street, the Dainty Dinah Tearooms are open from 10am daily, serving a wide range of hot and cold food and drinks, including great sandwiches, salads, jacket potatoes and delicious cakes.

3250

38740

8199

Right: Old photo of Rowley station *c* 1913
Below: Brass tidy made from No 178 Engine after collision near Otterington in 1892

The North East led the world in the development of railways. By 1880, the North Eastern Railway Company owned a network of lines covering Northumberland, County Durham and North Yorkshire, and was the lifeline for many small towns and villages.

The **Beamish Station** is a typical country station, as it would have been about 1913. Approaching from the town, a wrought-iron footbridge from Howden-le-Wear, takes visitors across the railway line towards the signal box, which came from Carr House East, Consett and dates from 1896.

The passenger station was first built in 1867, and came from Rowley, a village near Consett. The Station never had gas or electricity and was always lit by oil.

NER "C" Class locomotive No 876 of 1889 This locomotive was built at Gateshead in 1889 to the designs of T W Worsdell and it is an important part of the region's railway heritage. The type was used for passenger and freight throughout the North East. The Beamish example is the sole survivor of the 201 built. After many vicissitudes it was saved by Frank Atkinson and was even steamed at the museum in the late 1970s. The locomotive

K Hoole

JB

is at present away from the museum being assessed for a condition report.

The museum would like to restore the engine to full working order and an appearance in keeping with the period of its working life. It is hoped to make this remarkable veteran available for operation at as many suitable locations as possible throughout the North of England, acting as an ambassador for the museum in the process.

Top: The Regional Museums Store built to represent the Beamish Waggon and Iron Works
Above: Brass snuff box of 1854

Left and below: Works plate from renumbered NER Class "C" loco of 1889 and old photo of this loco taken May 7th 1960 at Darlington

RMS

The Regional Museums Store is a joint initiative by Beamish and Tyne and Wear Museums. It is a huge warehouse, which contains a wide range of unique artefacts that represents the region's rich social, industrial, maritime, transport and agricultural heritage.

Some of the objects are very large, and many would have been scrapped if the museums had not rescued them. The Regional Museums Store provides a secure, permanent home and holds the objects in trust for future generations. Visitors to Beamish are able to see some of the collections from a viewing gallery. Occasional guided tours of the building are also available. Visitors are asked to remember that this is a store of industrial objects; many await restoration and may be dirty.

Regional Museums Store

Trams and Transport

Left, from top to bottom: Replica of Northern General bus; Blackpool 31 Tram of 1901; Horse drawn dogcart; Replica Armstrong Whitworth car
Right: Sunderland 16 tram of 1900

By the end of the 19th century, the growing towns and cities of the region needed a cheap and efficient transport system. At first horse-drawn omnibuses were used and then horse-drawn trams. Steam trams never really took off. From the late 1890s, electric tramways were developed across the region. The Beamish tramway has been operating for over 30 years. Visitors can now experience a tramcar ride on the most extensively worked heritage tramway in the UK – the result of a remarkable partnership between the museum and a small group of dedicated volunteers.

The Beamish fleet consists of six restored trams: Blackpool 31 was built in 1901 and was in service there until 1984. Sheffield 264 dates back to 1907 and operated until 1956. This tram is not running at present and is due to be thoroughly overhauled. Tram 196 is a foreigner originating in Oporto. Built to a pre-First World War design, it has been painted in the Gateshead livery.

Gateshead 10, one of three local trams

M828

in the Beamish fleet, was built in 1925 and remained in service until 1951. Newcastle 114 was built in 1901 for the opening of the Newcastle Corporation Tramway, was sold to Sheffield in 1940 and was eventually withdrawn from service in the early 1950s. It was discovered by the museum being used as a henhouse on a farm near Scunthorpe and was carefully restored to working condition in 1996. Sunderland 16 was built in 1900, substantially modified after the First World War, ceased running in 1954, after which the body was used as a farm toolshed.

A replica bus runs between the Town and the Colliery Village. It is based on a type used by Northern General Transport Co Ltd – a subsidiary of Gateshead tramways. In 1913 they operated 27 buses of which 17 were Daimler CC double deckers, the last to arrive being J2503. The replica Armstrong Whitworth car was specially built for Beamish and carries passengers also from the Town to the Colliery.

80212

3390

From top to bottom:
Oporto 196 tram pre-First World War; Newcastle 114 tram of 1901; Gateshead 10 tram of 1925

REA

Below left: Pre-1914 Traffic sign
Below: Sheffield 264 tram of 1907
Right: Old photo of Sunderland Corporation 15 tram with crew

M852

Home Farm

Below: Home Farm, once part of the Beamish Estate
Below middle: Blacksmith at work
Bottom: Staffordshire plate with the Durham Ox

Agriculture was, and is, an important industry in the region; new ideas in livestock breeding were pioneered in the North East. **Home Farm** was once part of the Beamish Estate, owned by the Eden

80412

and Shafto families. John Eden was a prominent member of the Royal Agricultural Society in the early 1800s and ensured that many new ideas of agriculturalists were introduced here. The farm was originally managed by a bailiff and maintained as a 'model farm'.

About 1799 a horse gin and barn thresher were installed, an important step in agriculture from hand to horsepower. Around 1850 the foldyards were developed and a steam engine replaced the horses as a source of power.

AGRICULTURAL IMPLEMENTS

List No. 111.

W. Summerscales & Sons, Ltd.,
Coney Lane Works,
KEIGHLEY.

The heart of the farm kitchen is a large range by Moffat of Gateshead and long farmhouse table where the family as well as farm labourers were fed. Oatbread hangs up above the range on a flake.

Locally made furniture can be seen here. Next door is the farm office and pantry leading to a dairy where butter and cheese would have been made.

Buildings around the farm include a combined pigsty and hen house. The pigs provided both warmth and protection from predators for the hens. Across the road, beside the

Above: Making bread in the kitchen at Home Farm
Below: Brass milk churn
Below right: Threshing Day at Low Waskerley Farm, Shotley Field

duckpond, is a bull hemmel and a corrugated-iron cattle shelter, one of the first of its kind when exhibited at the Royal Show in 1908.

Beamish keeps the breeds of farm livestock which were typical of northern farming – some of these are now rare breeds.

96337

24475

1913

Right: Heavy horses
ploughing
Below: Saddleback pigs
Bottom: Advertisement
for Thorley's cattle food
Below right: Heavy
horses in the yard at
Home Farm

80435

THORLEY'S

FOOD FOR CATTLE.

24116a

Some animals will be found in fields
around the museum or in pens in the
buildings. Our stock is cared for using
modern methods by specialist trained staff
under the guidance of the museum's
veterinary advisor. Animal
breeds include Shorthorn
cattle (descendants of the
famous Durham Ox),
Teeswater sheep,
Saddleback pigs, Clydesdale
horses, Dales ponies and
Cleveland Bay horses, now
very much a rare breed
under threat. Around the
farm will be seen a wide
range of geese, ducks
and farmyard poultry.
Throughout the year
our heavy horses can

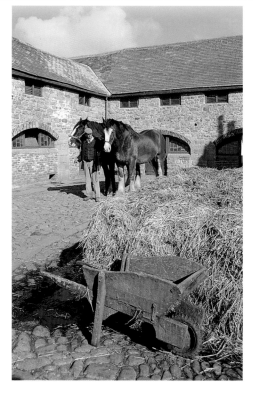

Above: Hay turning
Left: Print of The Blackwell Ox
Below: Teeswater sheep
Bottom left: Trade catalogue

be seen hard at work cultivating the fields around the museum. A ploughing match is held once a year, when ploughmen from all over England compete against each other in 'general purpose' or 'high cut' ploughing. Some splendid heavy horses in their decorated show harness can also be seen.

Canny Cuppa
TEA & COFFEE SNACKS TOILETS
HOME FARM EXHIBITION THIS WAY

T. CARRICK WATSON & SON, Tea Dealers & Coffee Roasters, &c.
17 to 21, Blackett Street, Newcastle.
CAFÉ
17, BLACKETT STREET.
LARGE AND WELL VENTILATED SMOKE ROOM.
SCIENTIFIC TRIUMPH IN COFFEE ROASTING.
SEE THE MACHINE WORKING as you go to the CAFÉ, 17, Blackett Street,
T. CARRICK WATSON & SON.

After a climb up the short hill to Home Farm, you'll probably be ready for a stop at the Canny Cuppa. Offering a range of light snacks, ice cream, tea and coffee and a wide range of chilled drinks, the Canny Cuppa is ideally situated close to Home Farm.

The Colliery Village

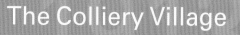

No recreation of the history of the North East would be complete without a colliery and the people who worked and lived in and around it. The extraction and use of coal powered this region. At its peak, in 1913, the Great Northern Coalfield employed nearly a quarter of a million men and boys, producing over 56 million tons of coal annually from about 400 pits.

Towns such as Seaham Harbour, West Hartlepool and Bedlington owed their very existence to coal.

Mining changed the landscape, the patterns of settlement and the traditions and way of life of the region.

Above: The Colliery Village, with pit cottages, Board School and chapel Below left: Pip the pit pony, now retired

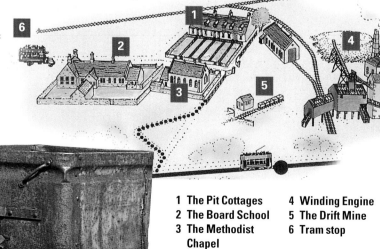

1 **The Pit Cottages**
2 **The Board School**
3 **The Methodist Chapel**
4 **Winding Engine**
5 **The Drift Mine**
6 **Tram stop**

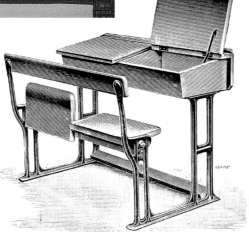

Pit communities are distinctive even today though they are rapidly disappearing.

The Colliery Village at Beamish is built around a recreation of a typical pit as it would have been in the early 1900s. A row of pit cottages, an engine shed, a tall stone engine house, together with a Board School and a Methodist chapel, have been carefully dismantled and rebuilt here. All have been saved from various parts of the region.

BURYS CELEBRATED PATENT PICKS

LION
BROAD EYE
SOLDIER
NARROW EYE

SHEFFIELD

Top right: Old photo from Huwood's mining machinery collection
Above right: Enamel advert for miners' picks
Above: Francis Street pit cottages
Far right: Harvest festival in the chapel

JG 304/33

Above: Pit cottage in winter. Upcast shaft in foreground
Right: Mrs Dormand of West Cramlington possing c1900
Far right: Kitchen of No 3

33207

The Pit Cottages from Francis Street, Hetton-le-Hole were built in the 1860s for pitmen and their families. Houses and coal were provided free in exchange for labour. Pit communities were close knit, consisting of mutually dependent families. In 1913, miners' wages were comparatively high, so they could afford to indulge their taste for expensive furniture which is represented in the cottages.

The backyards incorporated 'netties' or earth closets, which were emptied weekly by nightsoil men. A stand-pipe, one for every six houses, provided water, that had to be fetched for

44634

1825 **Pockerley Manor**

Georgian landscape

Pockerley Waggonway

Steam Elephant and Puffing Billy

1913 **The Town**

Bank and Masonic Hall

Garage and Sweet Shop

Printer's and Sun Inn

Carriage House

Ravensworth Terrace

Music Teacher

Dentist and Solicitor

The Co-op and Dainty Dinah

The Station and RMS

Trams and Transport

1913 Home Farm

1913 **Colliery Village**

Pit Cottages

School and Chapel

The Colliery

each house by bucket. Pitmen were prodigious gardeners, breeders of animals and often gamblers. Leek growing, pigeon fancying and whippet racing were popular pastimes.

No 1 is the Colliery Office, where the pitmen would collect their fortnightly wages. No 2 is occupied by a strict Methodist, strongly teetotal, and next door in No 3 lives a Roman Catholic family. No 4 is altogether sparser, occupied by a miner's widow and her sons, the breadwinners of the family.

Galvanised tin baths hang in the back yards. The family – the pitman in particular – bathed in front of the kitchen range but did not believe in washing his back in case it weakened it!

**Top: Kitchen No 4 –
a poorer household.
Taking in washing and
making mats to support
the family
Above left: Pitman
having his bath
Above right: Old photo
from Shotley Bridge area.
Mat making and drinking
during the 1892 miners'
strike
Above: Patchwork
pottery plate**

The School and Chapel

804[?]

Top: The Kindergarten
Above: Beamish Board School originally from East Stanley
Right: Abacus in trade catalogue

No. 444.
ABACUS.

Size 23in. × 20in.

Mounted on Telescopic Stand.

Total height at highest point, 58in. at lowest point, 49in.

18 9.

back to throw ours of ls. extra.

Abacus on Telescopic stand, with sliding slate coated half-screen for Chalk-work.

80470

The Beamish Board School once stood in nearby East Stanley. It was first opened in 1892, and when it closed, nearly a century later, three classrooms were rebuilt at Beamish. They would have accommodated up to 200 children. At the turn of the century school attendance was compulsory; the school leaving age was 12 years. Bright pupils who reached basic levels in reading, writing and arithmetic (the three 'R's') often left school early in order to support their families.

Board schools were built to high architectural standards. They were light and airy, a necessary feature in an era of poor hygiene.

The purpose of education was to create law-abiding, useful citizens.

Children were taught to 'know their place' and to 'show respect for their betters'.

Learning was instilled by rote and repetition. Doing sums – pounds, shillings and pence – and chanting multiplication tables were daily rituals. As well as the three 'R's', instruction was given in geography, history, domestic science, needlework, music, religious knowledge, hygiene and exercise drill.

Discipline was strict, with the cane as the ultimate deterrent, though it was seldom used. The punishment book recorded all misdemeanours. Despite the best efforts of the Schoolboard men, children were often absent throughout outbreaks of typhoid, tuberculosis, diphtheria, measles, and scarlatina.

The playground provided healthy exercise. Here the children played conkers, marbles and hopscotch. Boolers, otherwise known as the girth and crook, were very popular, as were singing and skipping games, distinctive to each locality.

Pit Hill Methodist Chapel

Pit Hill Methodist Chapel was built in 1854 to serve the local mining and farming communities. Methodism flourished in the North East. Founded by John and Charles Wesley, Methodism encompassed several shades of opinion. Pit Hill represents the Wesleyans, sometimes regarded as more respectable than the Primitives who were fiercely radical and independent.

The chapel fulfilled distinct social and spiritual needs of its members. In addition to the many services, there were women's meetings, Bible classes, temperance groups, choirs and Sunday schools.

THOU GOD SEEST ME

HYMNS. 762 91

As the coal mines expanded so the chapel membership increased and the chapel was enlarged in 1876 and again in 1904. At a time when opportunities for education were limited, the chapel taught its members skills which they used and many became influential members of both the Liberal and Labour parties as well as the Trade Unions.

The usual Church festivals were celebrated and the chapel Anniversary and Sunday School Anniversary were also important, featuring special events, concerts, talks and magic lantern shows.

WESLEY

Top left: Pit Hill Chapel
Top right: Practising the harmonium
Above: Wesley Methodist Love Feast mug

1825 Pockerley Manor

Georgian landscape

Pockerley Waggonway

Steam Elephant and Puffing Billy

1913 The Town

Bank and Masonic Hall

Garage and Sweet Shop

Printer's and Sun Inn

Carriage House

Ravensworth Terrace

Music Teacher

Dentist and Solicitor

The Co-op and Dainty Dinah

The Station and RMS

Trams and Transport

1913 Home Farm

1913 Colliery Village

Pit Cottages

School and Chapel

The Colliery

In the **Colliery Yard** is the entrance to Mahogany Drift Mine, first opened in the 1850s and worked intermittently during the 19th century. It was re-opened in 1921 to serve Beamish Chophill Colliery. Visitors can walk into the seam underground to see and feel what miners' working conditions were like. Hewers, working an eight-hour shift, cut coal by hand or with compressed air coal cutters. Conditions were often dark and wet. Coal was shovelled into tubs which were pushed by putters to the main haulage road where pit ponies were used to haul a train to the surface.

Across the yard the engine shed houses a collection of industrial locomotives: Head Wrightson, *Coffee Pot* of 1873, *Lewin* 683 of 1877 and *Coffee Pot* of 1871, both of which worked at Seaham Harbour.

The tall stone engine house came from Beamish Colliery 2nd Pit, known as the Chophill. Its steam winding engine was built by J & G Joicey & Co, of Newcastle upon Tyne in 1855. This is now the sole survivor of a type of engine once common in the northern coal field. To the rear of the winding house is a jack engine, used to lower heavy equipment down the shaft. Adjoining the engine house is a wooden heapstead building and screens originally from Ravensworth Park Drift mine in Gateshead. Here cages were drawn up from the shaft beneath. Tubs were pulled clear and coal tipped onto the screens for sorting before being loaded onto the chauldron waggons below. The cages wound men as well as coal.

Following the 1862 Hartley Disaster in

Top right: Pay tins – the pitmen were paid every two weeks
Top: Undercutting coal at Hartley Main Colliery
Above: Bait time in Mahogany Drift Mine
Below: Shaft sinking at Wallsend Colliery 1894

Below left and right: Davy type lamp *c* 1840 and Patterson's safety lamp *c* 1910
Far right: Winding engine of 1855 by Joicey of Newcastle

Right: Winding engine house, screens and Malleable No 5 loco *c* 1880 built by Grange Iron Works, Durham

Northumberland, legislation stated that all new pits must have two shafts to provide a means of escape in an emergency.

The winch from Silksworth Colliery was used when shafts were being sunk or widened. At the edge of the wood, beyond the winding engine house is a small powder house from Houghton Colliery used to store explosives for use underground.

Mining was a dangerous occupation. Roof falls, fires, explosions, suffocating gases and inundations were some of the hazards which took many lives. Our school's logbook records "Many of our children have lost fathers or brothers. The intense grief is unbearable. So few were present that we did not mark the register". The Burns Pit at West Stanley Colliery had exploded killing 168 men and boys in 1909.

80449

Clockwise from top left: 68th Regiment of Foot at Pockerley; two scenes from the National Traction Engine Trust; Best Decorated Horse; May Day Festivities; Great War Society event; threshing by steam

RJH

RJH

REA 1168/3

Throughout the summer
season, a variety of
historically linked, additional
events are held in appropriate
settings at Beamish. The
events may change from year
to year. In the past they have
included demonstrations by
the 68th Regiment of Light
Infantry and the Great War
Society. Vintage collections
and special car events are
held and there is a Cleveland
Bay Horse Day, and an
Annual Ploughing Match
with heavy horses at work.
Numerous other events such
as quilting and lacemaking
weekends are also held.

RJH

Beamish's educational work provides a variety of services, for a wide variety of audiences. A schools' programme of activities and resources is designed to meet the needs of the National Curriculum, GCSE, GNVQ and 'AS' and 'A' levels. Beamish hosts INSET days throughout the year, some in conjunction with Education Business Partnerships and LEA Advisors.

A busy hands-on activities programme throughout the year makes effective use of the museum's exhibits. Victorian lessons in the Board School, Pit cottage role play, Murder Mystery and Christmas at Home Farm are a few of these. From November to March, educational groups have the exclusive use of Pockerley Manor, where tallow candle making, baking and making heather brooms, give an experience

Pictures on this page: Role play activities in areas around the museum site

SH

of life as an 1820s servant. There is an additional charge for pupils undertaking these activities and the Education Department is happy to provide details.

Older pupils studying Leisure and Tourism or Business Studies are able to visit the museum as part of their course. Special needs are always addressed and there are considerable opportunities for Lifelong Learning. The recreation of 'Life as it was' allows great teaching and learning opportunities for people of all ages. First hand experience of sights, sounds, smells and tastes of the past provide a unique and unforgettable understanding of our heritage.

**Above: Pupils learning about the tram
Left and below left: At Home in the pit cottages
Below: Looking at changes in the landscape**

SH

The Collections

One of the most remarkable and fascinating features of Beamish is its collections. A policy of unselective collecting pursued in the museum's early years resulted in a wealth of material relating to the regional history being collected.

The Resource Collections are particularly important. They provide the information and research on which the period areas are based. These collections encompass a vast photographic archive of thousands of photographs, old and modern, illustrating people at work and play, regional scenes and buildings, as well as objects in the collections.

The Printed Book Collection consists of some 64,000 published books of the late 18th, 19th and 20th centuries, a magnificent collection of trade catalogues of suppliers and manufacturers, posters and ephemera, together forming a comprehensive reference source.

An Oral History Collection of recordings preserves the memories of many people from this region and is invaluable in recording historical facts, family information, stories, dialect and music.

30764

The Object Collections are vast. They include all aspects of social and domestic life, farming and rural life, industrial and town life as well as transport, all relating to the North East region. The collections are not limited by date but cover periods from the 1600s until the present day. The museum is still looking for further acquisitions, though selectively to fill gaps in certain areas.
Visit *www.beamishcollections.com*

PELAW LIQUID GRATE POLISH GRATO

NATIONAL HOUSEHOLD MILK MACHINE SKIMMED

PACKING OF RESPIRATOR.

SOCIALISM.

39543

Plain tree House,

ARSENIC

57124

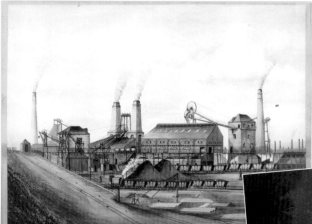

61922

A new **Regional Resource Centre** was officially opened in 2001, which now houses the Museum's huge core collections. The building has been designed and built to ensure that our regional treasures are stored and cared for in optimum conditions and for easy access to them.

A state-of-the-art roller racking system provides storage for thousands of artefacts in a controlled environment. A friendly search room is available to all, by appointment, providing facilities for research and for our collections to be viewed by computer.

28239

28998

32435

Regional Museums Store

In 1998 Beamish and Tyne & Wear Museums formed a strategic partnership to build a new store, providing accommodation for the large object collections from both museums. The long term care and very existence of many of these objects was under threat because of adverse conditions. The proposal received support from the Heritage Lottery Fund, the Designation Challenge Fund and North East Museums.

Amongst the most difficult items to move into the new store was the Tyne Wherry boat, Elswick No 2. The vessel is 7.4 metres wide and was built by R B Harrison and Son Ltd of Bill Quay, Gateshead in 1930. These boats carried materials and goods up and down the Tyne throughout the 19th and early 20th centuries.

The largest object to be moved into the store was the huge Doxford marine engine, designed to drive a ship's propeller. It weighs 125 tonnes and its power output is 4050 kw (5,500 horsepower). The engine was built in 1977 by Doxford Engines of Pallion, Sunderland. It was never installed in a ship, but was kept at the works for research and development.

REA 171/4

The store also accommodates other fascinating exhibits acquired over the years; the wooden vernacular boat collection of Tyne & Wear; a large engineering collection; railway rolling stock of the North Eastern Railway as well as collections of horse drawn vehicles and farm carts.

A huge collection of enamel adverts adorn the walls. Some of these collections will be used for future projects.

Regular open days are held throughout the year. Places must be booked in advance by contacting the Collections Access Officer on 0191 370 4050.

Friends of Beamish

The Friends of Beamish have supported the museum since the 1960s. Members come from all walks of life, and from throughout Britain and overseas with the common purpose of wishing to see the museum grow and to preserve their heritage.

Some Friends support by donating their subscription, whilst others prefer to be directly involved as volunteers using their skills to restore exhibits such as horsedrawn vehicles, bicycles, engines and farm equipment. Some work behind the scenes, assisting the museum staff in cataloguing library books and in documentation of the collections.

An increasing number work in costume assisting the demonstrators with interpretation in the period areas, and helping with special events. A specialist group of skilled engineers works on the tramway and another group advises on historic gardening.

The Friends' subscriptions pay for restoration and also for purchases for the museum. Friends receive a regular newsletter to help them keep in touch with recent developments, as well as free admission to Beamish throughout the year. There is an active programme of talks by visiting speakers, during the winter season.

The Friends of Beamish is a Registered Charity (No 1059957) and a Limited Company. Its Registered Office is at The Friends Office, Beamish, The North of England Open Air Museum, Beamish, Co. Durham DH9 0RG.

Telephone: 0191 370 1104
Web site: www.friendsofbeamish.co.uk
E-mail: info@friendsofbeamish.co.uk

Beamish

30081

For over 30 years, Beamish has been recognised as a great place for a day out. What you may not realise is there is much more to Beamish than meets the eye. From annual membership schemes to special daytime and evening events, we offer a wide range of additional opportunities to help you, your family, your friends and even your company or organisation to get the most out of Beamish.

The Beamish Club

Visitors who live permanently in Northumberland, Tyne & Wear, County Durham and the Cleveland/Tees Valley can now enjoy the magic of Beamish time and time again by joining 'The Beamish Club', one of the largest membership schemes of any museum in the United Kingdom. For an annual one-off fee, members can enjoy as many visits as they wish, completely free of charge.

REA 157/13

8224

Event Hosting

Beamish is gaining a reputation for exceptional event opportunities. From major product launches to small dinner parties, corporate 'family days' to family anniversaries, we can offer unique locations and tailored catering packages to make your event, no matter how big or small, a real success.

If it's a venue for a meeting that you're after, we have conference facilities overlooking The Town for up to 70 delegates. Additionally our Events Field is used as a base for a wide range of high profile corporate and charity events throughout the year. By holding your event at Beamish, you'll be giving your customers or staff the benefit of a memorable (and full) day out at our multi-award-winning Museum.

Beamish really comes into its own for evening events, using some of our most popular buildings which can be converted to suit your needs. Think for a moment about the magic of Pockerley Manor & Waggonway, Home Farm, The Sun Inn pub and The Carriage House – all of which are full of character. In short, we can work with you to develop your ideas into something really special.

To give you a flavour of what we can do, here are just a few examples of our current bookings:

- **Family days** (for organisations large and small)
- **Charity fundraising events**
- **Training courses**
- **Product launches**
- **Wedding anniversaries**
- **Retirement evenings**
- **Awards ceremonies**
- **Special evening receptions**
- **Photo shoots and filming**
- **Dinner parties**

If you'd like to know more, simply call our Events team on 0191 370 4000

YL 2328

Not only that, but members may also bring a limited number of guests with them at much reduced admission rates.

If you are interested in joining, simply call 0191 370 3131 with your credit card details, or pick up an application form at our Entrance Building.

For visitors wishing to take a more active role in the restoration and operational side of the museum, or for those living outside the areas listed above, why not join 'The Friends of Beamish'. Further details can be found on page 61.

REA 132/7

Saving the past for the future – Beamish Development Trust

We all need to feel connected to history – to the past lives of our families, our neighbourhoods, our region.

Yet forty years ago the buildings, machinery and objects that have given the North of England its distinct identity were in danger of vanishing for ever.

Today Beamish is the treasure-house of the region and England's finest open air museum of social, industrial and agricultural history.

As one of the North's major tourist attractions, with over 320,000 visitors annually, Beamish also makes a major contribution to employment and the regeneration of the region.

More than 96% of the Museum's running costs of £4m a year are met by admissions charges, the remainder coming from the region's local authorities. Funds for improvements and new historic features must come from grants and donations.

The Beamish Development Trust is a registered charity which encourages support from individuals, companies and charitable trusts to help the museum to grow. Money raised by the Trust can be used as matched funding for European and Lottery grants. Important new features such as the period Barclays Bank in the Town, Pockerley Manor and the 1825 area, and the replica locomotives, have been funded in this way.

There is more to be done. The Museum has ambitious plans for further development to increase our understanding of the region's past. The Beamish Vision encompasses a new visitor centre with space to permanently display more of the Museum's superb collections, an education centre and better visitor facilities, as well as additions to all the period areas and new ways to make the most of the beautiful and historic landscape of the Beamish Valley.

The Trust also raises funds to enable local schools and disadvantaged groups to visit the Museum. Proceeds from the annual Beamish Tram Challenge, where runners race a tram around the museum site, go towards this cause.

All this is only possible through the support of people both within the region and outside who regard Beamish with affection and pride.

Many local companies show their support, either by joining Business@Beamish, our corporate membership scheme, or by holding corporate events here. Business@Beamish entitles members to a range of benefits for a one off fee including a Family Day for staff, use of Beamish facilities and special events. There is also a range of sponsorship opportunities.

There are many ways for individuals to help, including Gift Aid donations, gifts of shares, and donations of items for the collections. Legacies and in memoriam gifts are especially welcome. These can be dedicated to a particular area of the museum and can provide a permanent memorial to a benefactor's name. We are happy to discuss the particular wishes of donors.

If you would like to play your part in bringing the region's past to life and safeguarding its future, by making a donation or leaving a bequest in your will, please write to Beamish Development Trust, Beamish, Co Durham, DH9 0RG, phone 0191 370 4021, or visit www.beamish.org.uk